Choose Love

STORMIE OMARTIAN

HARVEST HOUSE PUBLISHERS
EUGENE, OREGON

Cover by Harvest House Publishers, Inc., Eugene, Oregon

Back cover author photo © Michael Gomez Photography

Italics in quoted Scriptures indicate emphasis added by the author.

CHOOSE LOVE BOOK OF PRAYERS
Copyright © 2014 by Stormie Omartian
Published by Harvest House Publishers
Eugene, Oregon 97402
www.harvesthousepublishers.com

ISBN 978-0-7369-5991-9 (pbk.)
ISBN 978-0-7369-5992-6 (eBook)

Printed in the United States of America

14 15 16 17 18 19 20 21 / BP-JH / 10 9 8 7 6 5 4 3 2 1

Introduction

~~~~~~

God is love. And He wants us to become more like Him. But how do we love others the way He does? Do we have the energy, strength, and purity of heart to have love that is unconditional and unfailing? Do we naturally have love that is always long-suffering and kind? Do we have love that is never envious, prideful, rude, selfish, or easily provoked? Do we have love that always bears, believes, hopes, and endures all things? Do we have love that never fails?

All of that is impossible without the love of God flowing powerfully in us at all times. In order to have that, we first of all need to understand how much He loves us. And we do that by choosing to open up to His love by reading

His Word—His love letter to us—and also receiving His greatest gift of love to us, His Son, Jesus. Second, we must let our love for *Him* grow and express it to Him more and more each day. The third choice we must make is to show His perfect love in us to others in a way that pleases Him.

It's my prayer that this little *Choose Love Book of Prayers* will help you to do all of that, so you can receive the blessings that are there for you when you obey the Lord and love others as He loves you.

— Stormie Omartian —

Beloved, let us love one another,
for love is of God;
and everyone who loves
is born of God and knows God.

1 John 4:7

1

See Yourself
the Way God Sees You

~~~~~~

Lord, help me to see myself the way You see me. Thank You that You see me through Your eyes of love and all You created me to be. Enable me to open up my heart to receive Your love. Although it's hard to comprehend a love so great, and I don't feel worthy of it, I don't want to shut myself off from the power of Your amazing love working in my heart. Give me eyes to see how You reveal Your love for me by keeping me from things that are not Your greatest good for my life. I know that everything You want to do in my life cannot be accomplished without Your love flowing in me.

In Jesus' name I pray.

O LORD, You have searched me and known me.
You know my sitting down and my rising up;
You understand my thought afar off.

PSALM 139:1-2

Prayer Notes

_____

_____

_____

_____

_____

_____

_____

_____

_____

_____

_____

_____

2

See Yourself
the Way God Sees You

~~~~~~

*L*ord, help me turn my gaze from myself to You. I want to see You more clearly and understand You more fully. Thank You that You not only love me, but You will enable me to understand the depth of Your love. Show me the ways I don't recognize or open up to Your love—whether because of serious doubt or simply a lack of understanding—and I have missed many of Your blessings because of it. I know You see all my ways and count all my steps, and You know me better than I know myself. Help me to recognize the ways You show Your love to me because I am Your child.

In Jesus' name I pray.

We know that the Son of God has come
and has given us an understanding, that we may
know Him who is true; and we are in Him
who is true, in His Son Jesus Christ.

1 JOHN 5:20

Prayer Notes

_____

_____

_____

_____

_____

_____

_____

_____

_____

_____

_____

3

See Yourself
the Way God Sees You

~~~~~~

Lord, enable me to see my life from Your perspective. Instead of looking through a magnifying lens to see the flaws in myself, help me to see through the magnifying lens of Your loving heart to observe the good—and potential for greatness—you have put in me. May Your presence be magnified in my life beyond what I can even imagine now. Cause Your perfection, beauty, love, and holiness to be reflected in me at all times. Enable me to fully receive Your love. I want to not just read about it or think about it; I want to experience it. Help me to walk so closely with You that I feel it every day.

In Jesus' name I pray.

His divine power has given to us all things that pertain to life and godliness, through the knowledge of Him who called us by glory and virtue.

2 Peter 1:3

Prayer Notes

_____

_____

_____

_____

_____

_____

_____

_____

_____

_____

_____

_____

4

Understand Who
God Really Is

~~~~~~

*L*ord, I long to know You better. Teach me all about You. I know I cannot begin to comprehend Your greatness without Your opening my eyes, enlarging my heart and mind, and giving me revelation. "O Lord my God, You are very great: You are clothed with honor and majesty, who cover Yourself with light as with a garment, who stretch out the heavens like a curtain" (Psalm 104:1-2). Help me to understand all that You are so that I can grow ever deeper in my walk with You. You are the all-knowing Creator of all things, and You can transform anyone with Your love if they will receive it. I open my heart fully to You and ask You to transform me.

In Jesus' name I pray.

Show me Your ways, O Lord; teach me Your paths.
Lead me in Your truth and teach me,
for You are the God of my salvation;
on You I wait all the day.

PSALM 25:4-5

Prayer Notes

_____

_____

_____

_____

_____

_____

_____

_____

_____

_____

_____

5

Understand Who God Really Is

~~~~~~

*L*ord, enable me to comprehend all that You do. Help me to remember at all times that You never change. You are who You are, and no lies of the enemy can alter that in any way. "Your throne is established from of old; You are from everlasting" (Psalm 93:2). "You, LORD, are most high above all the earth; You are exalted far above all gods" (Psalm 97:9). I pray that the essence and character of who You are will transform me and guide who I become. Thank You that You are a good God and everything You do is good. Because You are the God of love, I know everything You do in my life is because You love me.

In Jesus' name I pray.

LORD, You have been our dwelling place
in all generations.
Before the mountains were brought forth,
or ever You had formed the earth
and the world, even from everlasting
to everlasting, You are God.

PSALM 90:1-2

Prayer Notes

_____

_____

_____

_____

_____

_____

_____

_____

_____

_____

_____

6

Understand Who God Really Is

~~~~~~

Lord, I cannot fathom Your *love* for me without understanding all You have *done* for me. Enable me to fully open my heart and mind to receive that wonderful knowledge of You. Thank You that Your love is unconditional, unchanging, and unfailing. Teach me to understand and acknowledge all the ways You demonstrate Your love toward me. Fortify my spirit so I never doubt it. Help me trust at all times that Your love is real and true and always there for me in unlimited supply. Thank You that You are all-powerful and nothing is impossible for You. Thank You that You are all-seeing and You know everything about me. Thank You that Your loving-kindness and goodness toward me never fail.

In Jesus' name I pray.

Hope does not disappoint, because the love of God has been poured out in our hearts by the Holy Spirit who was given to us.

ROMANS 5:5

Prayer Notes

_____

_____

_____

_____

_____

_____

_____

_____

_____

_____

_____

7

Receive All
God Has for You

~~~~~~

*L*ord, I realize I can never receive all You *have* for me until I understand everything You *did* for me. Thank You that You, "the ruler over the kings of the earth," loved me enough to wash me clean of all my sins by Your own blood (Revelation 1:5). Thank You that You are the living Word. You are my Savior. You have set me free from the consequences of my own sins, errors, mistakes, and ignorance. And You have made me to be a beloved child of God. Thank You that receiving Your love for me has caused my life to finally make sense. Thank You that in You I find everything I need for life (1 Corinthians 8:6).

In Jesus' name I pray.

For us there is one God, the Father,
of whom are all things, and we for Him;
and one Lord Jesus Christ,
through whom are all things,
and through whom we live.

1 Corinthians 8:6

Prayer Notes

_____

_____

_____

_____

_____

_____

_____

_____

_____

_____

8

Receive All
God Has for You

~~~~~~

*L*ord, thank You that You came "as a light into the world" so that I would never have to live in darkness (John 12:46). Thank You for Your Holy Spirit in me, for Your Word says that "if anyone does not have the Spirit of Christ, he is not His" (Romans 8:9). But You have given me Your Spirit when I received You, and He is the seal and sign that I am Yours and You are with me always. Because of all You have done for me, I will live eternally with You and no one can change that. You are my Savior, Redeemer, and Restorer. Upon You I have established the foundation of my life.

In Jesus' name I pray.

In this the love of God was manifested toward us, that God has sent His only begotten Son into the world, that we might live through Him.

1 John 4:9

Prayer Notes

_____

_____

_____

_____

_____

_____

_____

_____

_____

9

Receive All
God Has for You

~~~~~~

Lord, thank You that You share Yourself with me.
You share Your love, peace, and power. You
share Your Spirit and Your wholeness. You are the
bread of heaven who feeds me life. You are the
fountain of living water in me that never runs dry.
You are the way, the truth, and the life. You are my
foundation (1 Corinthians 3:11). You are the living
Word and the door to eternal life. You are the good
shepherd, and I hear the voice of Your Spirit leading me. Thank You that You are unchanging and I
can forever depend on You (Hebrews 13:8). Help
me to never forget the extent of all You have done
for me because You love me.

In Jesus' name I pray.

*In Him dwells all the fullness of the Godhead bodily;
and you are complete in Him.*

COLOSSIANS 2:9-10

Prayer Notes

_____

_____

_____

_____

_____

_____

_____

_____

_____

_____

10

Read God's
Love Letter to You

~~~~~~

*L*ord, thank You for Your Word. I know it's Your love letter to me because every time I read or speak it, I experience Your presence and love in a deeper way. It feeds my soul and makes my life rich. Help me to understand it better every day. "Open my eyes, that I may see wondrous things from Your law" (Psalm 119:18). Help me to know You in greater depth through it. Thank You that Your Word gives me truth and guidance for my life. Help me to always keep Your Word in my heart and not forget it. Make the Scriptures come alive to me every time I read them. Keep them alive in me at all times.

In Jesus' name I pray.

*The statutes of the LORD are right,
rejoicing the heart;
the commandment of the LORD is pure,
enlightening the eyes.*

PSALM 19:8

Prayer Notes

_____

_____

_____

_____

_____

_____

_____

_____

_____

_____

Read God's
Love Letter to You

~~~~~~

*L*ord, thank You that Your Word is perfect and it changes me every time I read it. All Your laws and commandments are right and are there for my benefit as boundaries to keep me protected and safe. Thank You for the blessings I receive when I obey them. Your Word brings me peace and a sense of well-being. "Your testimonies also are my delight and my counselors" (Psalm 119:24). Help me to clearly hear You speak to me as I read Your Word. Thank You for Your commands, rules, and laws, for they are there to guide me. And when I follow them, I get to where I need to go and my life is far better.

In Jesus' name I pray.

As for God, His way is perfect;
the word of the LORD is proven;
He is a shield to all who trust in Him.

PSALM 18:30

Prayer Notes

_____

_____

_____

_____

_____

_____

_____

_____

_____

_____

12

Read God's
Love Letter to You

~~~~~~

*L*ord, I am grateful You always keep Your Word. I know I can faithfully take You at Your Word and it will never fail me. You are the living Word, Jesus, and You have magnified Your Word above all Your name (Psalm 138:2). Etch it on my heart in a lasting and life-changing way. Weave it into the fabric of my being so that it becomes part of me. Help me to see Your love for me on every page. Each day I read it I pray You will penetrate my heart and mind, and open both so You can bring about the changes in me that are needed. Thank You that Your Word makes wise the simple, rejoices the heart, and enlightens the eyes (Psalm 19:7-8).

In Jesus' name I pray.

Your word I have hidden in my heart,
that I might not sin against You.

PSALM 119:11

Prayer Notes

_____

_____

_____

_____

_____

_____

_____

_____

_____

_____

_____

13

Accept God's
Grace and Mercy

~~~~~~

*L*ord, thank You for Your grace and mercy, which I know are never-ending signs of Your unfailing love for me. They are gifts beyond comprehension. For it is You who redeems my life from destruction and crowns me "with lovingkindness and tender mercies" (Psalm 103:4). Thank You that You care about the things I care about. Thank You that You "will perfect that which concerns me; Your mercy, O LORD, endures forever" (Psalm 138:8). That means I can always depend on it. Thank You that because I have received Jesus I have been forgiven, but You have promised to forgive even the sins I commit in the future when I come to You with a repentant heart and confess them.

In Jesus' name I pray.

*"With everlasting kindness
I will have mercy on you,"*
says the LORD, your Redeemer.

ISAIAH 54:8

Prayer Notes

_____

_____

_____

_____

_____

_____

_____

_____

_____

_____

_____

14

Accept God's
Grace and Mercy

~~~~~~

Lord, thank You for Your forgiveness. I can't imagine the condition of my life and the state of my soul without it. I know that guilt is a killer and condemnation destroys. I am forever grateful that when I recognize my own error and bad choices that have led me to stray from Your ways, I can come to You with a humble and repentant heart and You not only will forgive me, but You remove my transgressions as far as the east is from the west (Psalm 103:12). "Do not remember the sins of my youth, nor my transgressions; according to Your mercy remember me, for Your goodness' sake, O LORD" (Psalm 25:7). Your grace and mercy assure me of Your love.

In Jesus' name I pray.

God, who is rich in mercy, because of His great love with which He loved us, even when we were dead in trespasses, made us alive together with Christ (by grace you have been saved), and raised us up together, and made us sit together in the heavenly places in Christ Jesus.

EPHESIANS 2:4-6

Prayer Notes

_____

_____

_____

_____

_____

_____

_____

_____

_____

_____

_____

Accept God's Grace and Mercy

~~~~~~

Lord, thank You for the gift of Your grace that gives me what I don't deserve. Thank You for Your grace that drew me to put my faith in You and allowed me to be saved from death and eternity without You. Thank You that Your grace is the great manifestation of Your love for me, and Your mercy keeps me from being punished as I deserve. Thank You that Your goodness and mercy will follow me all the days of my life, and because of that I will live with You now and forever. Help me to keep myself in Your love, dwelling in the flow of Your mercy, even into heaven with You after I leave this earth (Jude 21).

In Jesus' name I pray.

Surely goodness and mercy shall
follow me all the days of my life;
and I will dwell in the house of the LORD forever.

PSALM 23:6

Prayer Notes

_____

_____

_____

_____

_____

_____

_____

_____

_____

_____

16

Recognize the Ways God Loves You

~~~~~~

Lord, thank You for all of the ways You love me. I recognize them more and more. I am so grateful that nothing will separate me from Your love. Thank You that Your Word promises to those in need that "in the days of famine" we will "be satisfied" (Psalm 37:19). I don't have to fear not having enough, and I can trust that because You are my Lord, I will not want for anything (Psalm 23:1). Thank You that You have a place of rest for me where there is fruitful abundance (Psalm 23:2). Thank You that You will not withhold any good thing from those who live Your way (Psalm 84:11).

In Jesus' name I pray.

Do not worry, saying, "What shall we eat?" or "What shall we drink?" or "What shall we wear?"... Your heavenly Father knows that you need all these things. But seek first the kingdom of God and His righteousness, and all these things shall be added to you.

MATTHEW 6:31-33

Prayer Notes

_____

_____

_____

_____

_____

_____

_____

_____

_____

17

Recognize the Ways God Loves You

~~~~~~

Lord, I know Your ways are perfect and You have proven Your Word time after time. I know You will always be a shield to me because I trust in You (Psalm 18:30). Thank You that *"You have been a shelter for me, a strong tower from the enemy. I will abide in Your tabernacle forever; I will trust in the shelter of Your wings"* (Psalm 61:3-4). "I will both lie down in peace, and sleep; for You alone, O LORD, make me dwell in safety" (Psalm 4:8). So many of the promises in Your Word, like these, assure me that You will provide for me in every way—all because You love me. I am grateful that You always keep Your promises.

In Jesus' name I pray.

The LORD will command
His lovingkindness in the daytime,
and in the night His song shall be with me—
a prayer to the God of my life.

PSALM 42:8

Prayer Notes

_____

_____

_____

_____

_____

_____

_____

_____

_____

_____

_____

_____

18

Recognize the Ways God Loves You

∿∿∿∿∿∿∿∿∿∿∿∿∿∿∿∿∿∿∿∿∿∿∿∿∿∿∿∿∿∿∿∿∿

Lord, thank You that You are "a God near at hand" and "not a God afar off" (Jeremiah 23:23). "You have also given me the shield of Your salvation; Your right hand has held me up, Your gentleness has made me great" (Psalm 18:35). "You, O God, have heard my vows; You have given me the heritage of those who fear Your name" (Psalm 61:5). "You have put gladness in my heart" (Psalm 4:7). I see Your love for me in the promises found in Your Word. Help me to recognize Your love for me—especially in the passages I am not yet seeing or understanding—and in all the ways You reveal Your love for me every day.

In Jesus' name I pray.

May your unfailing love be with us, LORD,
even as we put our hope in you.

PSALM 33:22 NIV

Prayer Notes

_____

_____

_____

_____

_____

_____

_____

_____

_____

_____

_____

Know What God's Love Will Do in Your Life

~~~~~~

Lord, I am amazed at what You *can* and *will* do in me because You love me. Help me to understand the expanse of Your reach into my life. Enable me to remember this when I am in the middle of a storm and need You to bring calm (Psalm 107:28-29). Thank You that You can turn a wilderness into a pool of refreshing water (Psalm 107:35). Thank You that You always see me and know where I am. I am grateful that because I have invited You to be Lord over my life, Your hand is always upon me and will guide me where I need to go. Thank You that because I am with You, You are always with me.

In Jesus' name I pray.

Whoever keeps His word,
truly the love of God is perfected in him.

1 John 2:5

Prayer Notes

_____

_____

_____

_____

_____

_____

_____

_____

_____

_____

_____

20

Know What God's Love
Will Do in Your Life

~~~~~~

*L*ord, I am grateful that because You love me, there is no place I can be that Your Spirit is not with me (Psalm 139:8-10). Thank You that You will never leave or forsake me, and even in old age I will always have a great purpose. Help me to abide in You so that I will always bear good fruit in my life. I know that without You I can do nothing good and lasting. Thank You that You will bring good out of bad situations if I walk closely with You, live Your way, and pray. Thank You that because You love me You will give me everything I need to live the life You have for me.

In Jesus' name I pray.

Search me, O God, and know my heart;
try me, and know my anxieties;
and see if there is any wicked way in me,
and lead me in the way everlasting.

PSALM 139:23-24

Prayer Notes

_____

_____

_____

_____

_____

_____

_____

_____

_____

_____

_____

21

Love Who He Is
Wholeheartedly

~~~~~~

Lord, I love who You are and all You have done for me. I love all Your promises to me, and everything You have planned for my future. Reveal to me any place in my life where I am not depending on You as should. I am eternally grateful to be an heir of Your kingdom that You have given to those who love You (James 2:5). But even more than all of that, I simply want to love You with all my *heart, soul, mind,* and *strength* just as You desire (Mark 12:30). Help me to love You with my entire being, without compromise. Teach me how to accomplish that in every way that is pleasing to You.

In Jesus' name I pray.

I love the LORD, because He has heard
my voice and my supplications.
Because He has inclined His ear to me,
therefore I will call upon Him as long as I live.

PSALM 116:1-2

Prayer Notes

_____
_____
_____
_____
_____
_____
_____
_____
_____
_____
_____

22

Love Who He Is Wholeheartedly

~~~~~~

*L*ord, I don't want to be like the Pharisees who tried to do everything perfectly—and legalistically—but bypassed the part about loving You (Luke 11:42). I know You see who has true love for You in their heart and who does not (John 5:42). I don't ever want You to see me offer You lukewarm or halfhearted love where You are concerned. I want to be able to show my adoration and consistently express my love for You in the most heartfelt ways. No one has ever loved me more than You. You are my greatest treasure and my heart is with You above all else. Help me to make room in my life for all that You are.

In Jesus' name I pray.

The LORD does not see as man sees;
for man looks at the outward appearance,
but the LORD looks at the heart.

1 Samuel 16:7

Prayer Notes

23

Love Who He Is Wholeheartedly

~~~~~~

Lord, Your Word says that if anyone loves You, that person is known by You (1 Corinthians 8:3). I want to be known by You in great depth, and to know You deeply as well. Help me to be "rooted and grounded in love" so that everything I do reflects my love for You (Ephesians 3:17). Thank You that You loved me long before I ever knew to love You (1 John 4:19). Now I love everything about You. Enable me to walk more closely to You every day so that I can know You better. Help me to love You more than anything in my life—more than people, possessions, and more than life itself—because nothing is greater than You.

In Jesus' name I pray.

Whom have I in heaven but You?
And there is none upon earth
that I desire besides You.

PSALM 73:25

Prayer Notes

_____

_____

_____

_____

_____

_____

_____

_____

_____

_____

_____

_____

24

Live His Way
Uncompromisingly

~~~~~~

*L*ord, I pray You would help me to live Your way without compromise. Teach me Your laws and commands so they are etched upon my heart. "Your word is a lamp to my feet and a light to my path" (Psalm 119:105). Guide me every day in the way I should go. Your laws are good and more desirable than fine gold, and You have a great reward for those who keep them (Psalm 19:9-11). Thank You that because I love Your ways, You have anointed me "with the oil of gladness" (Psalm 45:7). I know that sin of any kind in my life—for which I have not repented—causes You to not hear my prayers. Help me to repent quickly.

In Jesus' name I pray.

I have been crucified with Christ;
it is no longer I who live,
but Christ lives in me;
and the life which I now live in the flesh
I live by faith in the Son of God,
who loved me and gave Himself for me.

GALATIANS 2:20

Prayer Notes

_____

_____

_____

_____

_____

_____

_____

_____

_____

_____

_____

25

Live His Way
Uncompromisingly

~~~~~~

Lord, I love Your laws because I know they are right and they keep me from stumbling, and all who keep them have great peace (Psalm 119:165). I know that "all Your commandments are truth" and they have been true and unfailing forever (Psalm 119:151). "I rejoice at Your word as one who finds great treasure" (Psalm 119:162). Help me to always feel that way. Make my faith grow as I read and hear Your Word so that I can obey it fully (Romans 10:17). I know the one who keeps Your commands is the one who loves you (John 14:21). The connection between loving You and living Your way is clear. Help me never forget that.

In Jesus' name I pray.

Great peace have those who love Your law,
and nothing causes them to stumble.

PSALM 119:165

Prayer Notes

_____

_____

_____

_____

_____

_____

_____

_____

_____

_____

26

Live His Way Uncompromisingly

~~~~~~

Lord, I love Your ways and despise the ways of those who don't (Psalm 119:128). "Rivers of water run down from my eyes, because men do not keep Your law" (Psalm 119:136). It grieves me to see people disregard Your laws. I know it grieves You even more when I do the same. You see my "secret sins" and I don't ever want separation to come between You and me (Psalm 90:8). So I ask You to expose them if I am allowing something into my mind and heart that should not be there. I will confess it before You so that I can be forgiven and remove any separation between us. "You are my hiding place and my shield; I hope in Your word" (Psalm 119:114).

In Jesus' name I pray.

I have restrained my feet from every evil way,
that I may keep Your word.

PSALM 119:101

Prayer Notes

_____

_____

_____

_____

_____

_____

_____

_____

_____

_____

27

Learn to
Worship Him Lavishly

~~~~~~

Lord, I worship You for who You are, and I praise You for all You have done in my life. Teach me how to worship You lavishly with all that is in me. Help me to glorify Your name in worship always (Psalm 86:12). Your name alone is above all names and is exalted, and Your glory is "above the earth and heaven" (Psalm 148:13). Let Your high praise always be in my mouth and a two-edged sword in my hand (Psalm 149:6). Help me make praise and worship of You the first thing I do every day and the first way I deal with any problem in my life. You are always greater than anything I face.

In Jesus' name I pray.

Bless the LORD, O my soul;
and all that is within me, bless His holy name!

PSALM 103:1

Prayer Notes

_____

_____

_____

_____

_____

_____

_____

_____

_____

_____

28

Learn to
Worship Him Lavishly

~~~~~~

Lord, help me to never number my assets as David did to give glory to anyone or anything other than You as the source of all my blessings. Show me any place in my life where I am doing that. I don't want leanness to creep into my soul. I only want the fullness of life and heart that You have for me. Thank You that You satisfy my hungry soul with Your goodness (Psalm 107:8-9). I am always hungry for more of You in my life. Thank You that "in the day when I cried out, You answered me, and made me bold with strength in my soul" (Psalm 138:3). So I will praise You boldly as long as I live.

In Jesus' name I pray.

*It is good to give thanks to the LORD,
and to sing praises to Your name, O Most High;
to declare Your lovingkindness in the morning,
and Your faithfulness every night.*

PSALM 92:1-2

Prayer Notes

_____

_____

_____

_____

_____

_____

_____

_____

_____

_____

29

Learn to
Worship Him Lavishly

~~~~~~

Lord, I come before You with thanksgiving and worship only You. "You are my God, and I will praise You" and exalt You above all else (Psalm 118:28). I give You all the glory due You because You are worthy of praise. I worship You in the beauty of Your holiness (Psalm 29:2). I proclaim that this is the day You have made and I will rejoice and be glad in it (Psalm 118:24). "Be exalted, O God, above the heavens; let Your glory be above all the earth" (Psalm 57:11). I pray my worship of You will always be pleasing in Your sight. Teach me how to praise You lavishly with my whole heart.

In Jesus' name I pray.

I will sing to the LORD as long as I live;
I will sing praise to my God
while I have my being.
May my meditation be sweet to Him;
I will be glad in the LORD.

PSALM 104:33-34

Prayer Notes

_____

_____

_____

_____

_____

_____

_____

_____

_____

_____

30

Look for Ways to
Trust Him Completely

~~~~~~

*L*ord, I put my trust in You. I quiet my soul and wait for You to be my defense, and I will not allow myself to be moved or shaken (Psalm 62:1-2). Reveal any place in my heart where I am afraid to do that fully. Help me to put You first in everything I do—day and night. I pray to You as David did, "Give heed to the voice of my cry, my King and my God, for to You I will pray. My voice You shall hear in the morning, O LORD; in the morning I will direct it to You, and I will look up" (Psalm 5:2-3). Thank You that You hear my prayers and will answer.

In Jesus' name I pray.

You will keep him in perfect peace,
whose mind is stayed on You,
because he trusts in You.

ISAIAH 26:3

Prayer Notes

_____

_____

_____

_____

_____

_____

_____

_____

_____

_____

31

Look for Ways to Trust Him Completely

~~~~~~

Lord, help me to always look to You and not focus on my problems. Teach me to "pray without ceasing" (1 Thessalonians 5:17). My soul waits on You for answers to my prayers, because You are my help and shield (Psalm 33:20). I know that You will strengthen my heart when I put my hope in You (Psalm 31:24). I know there is peace to be found in any trial when I invite Your presence into it. Enable me to keep praying and seeking that peace in You until I have found it. Help me to trust in You with all that is within me and not trust in my own thoughts or those of anyone else.

In Jesus' name I pray.

Trust in the LORD with all your heart,
and lean not on your own understanding;
in all your ways acknowledge Him,
and He shall direct your paths.

PROVERBS 3:5-6

Prayer Notes

32

Look for Ways to Trust Him Completely

~~~~~~

Lord, I thank You for Your thoughts toward me, which "are more than can be numbered" (Psalm 40:5). I am constantly grateful that You love me. "Show me Your ways, O LORD; teach me Your paths...on You I wait all the day" (Psalm 25:4-5). I lift my eyes to You for You are my help, and I know that You will not allow me to fall (Psalm 121:1,3). Help me to refuse all doubt and fear and not allow my thoughts to cause anxiety about anything. In the face of obstacles, help me to be determined to trust You completely. Enable me to put my complete trust in You at all times no matter what is happening.

In Jesus' name I pray.

Show Your marvelous lovingkindness
by Your right hand,
O You who save those who trust in You.

PSALM 17:7

Prayer Notes

_____

_____

_____

_____

_____

_____

_____

_____

_____

_____

_____

33

Lean on His Wisdom
Enthusiastically

~~~~~~

Lord, I love that Your wisdom is eternal, true, and always perfect. Help me to seek out and depend on Your wisdom every day and not the wisdom of the world. I reverence You and thank You that Your wisdom in me begins there. Thank You that Your law is in my heart and will keep me from slipping. I seek Your wisdom for every day and every decision. Holy Spirit of wisdom, fill me afresh with Your wisdom so that I can always hear Your wise counsel spoken to my heart. I depend on Your counsel for all things. Teach me to value that all my days on earth so I may gain a heart of wisdom (Psalm 90:12).

In Jesus' name I pray.

The mouth of the righteous speaks wisdom,
and his tongue talks of justice.
The law of his God is in his heart;
none of his steps shall slide.

PSALM 37:30-31

Prayer Notes

_____

_____

_____

_____

_____

_____

_____

_____

_____

_____

_____

34

Lean on His Wisdom
Enthusiastically

~~~~~~

Lord, I know that the counsel of nations comes to nothing, but You bless the nation who proclaims You are Lord and who seeks Your wisdom—the people You have chosen for Your own inheritance (Psalm 33:11-12). Thank You that Your counsel stands forever (Psalm 33:11). I am grieved at how my nation has rejected Your godly wisdom. Bring us back to You, I pray. Only in You can we ever find the wisdom to make right decisions. I know that man, in the arrogance of his own self-proclaimed wisdom, comes to destruction, but I trust that Your wisdom can enable me to survive and thrive wherever You plant me. I am grateful that Your wisdom in me gives me life.

In Jesus' name I pray.

*The excellence of knowledge
is that wisdom gives life to those who have it.*

ECCLESIASTES 7:12

Prayer Notes

_____

_____

_____

_____

_____

_____

_____

_____

_____

_____

_____

35

Lean on His Wisdom
Enthusiastically

~~~~~~

*L*ord, I praise and worship You. And I thank You that my having great reverence for You is where Your wisdom in me begins. Help me to always love and value Your wisdom far above all earthly knowledge. There is nothing more valuable on earth than this. I seek Your wisdom above earthly wisdom, for I know that those who do that are blessed. I don't want to be like those who "hated knowledge and did not choose the fear of the LORD" for they could not enjoy Your presence and did not get their prayers answered (Proverbs 1:28-29). As for me, I lean totally, enthusiastically, and unwaveringly on Your wisdom because I love and trust You.

In Jesus' name I pray.

Wisdom is better than rubies,
and all the things one may desire
cannot be compared with her.

PROVERBS 8:11

Prayer Notes

_____

_____

_____

_____

_____

_____

_____

_____

_____

_____

_____

36

Leave the World of His Enemy Entirely

~~~~~~

*L*ord, help me to express my love for You by separating myself completely from anything that is not pleasant in Your sight. If the enemy of my soul has anything in me, reveal it to me now so I can be free of any influence he may have. If I have in any way attached my heart or thoughts to his ways—or have been drawn away from Your kingdom—show me so I can repent of it and come back to You and under Your protective covering. Thank You that when the enemy of my soul comes in like an overwhelming flood, Your Spirit will surround me with protection and resistance. That's why I turn my eyes on You only.

In Jesus' name I pray.

When the enemy comes in like a flood,
the Spirit of the LORD will lift up
a standard against him.

ISAIAH 59:19

Prayer Notes

_____

_____

_____

_____

_____

_____

_____

_____

_____

_____

37

Leave the World of His Enemy Entirely

~~~~~~

Lord, enable me to stand strong in resisting the enemy so he will flee from me. I will not look to any person to be my savior "for the help of man is useless" if not led by You (Psalm 108:12). Against the enemy, no one can do what You do. That's why my eyes are always on You (Psalm 25:15). Thank You, Jesus, that You have defeated the enemy and put him under Your feet. Help me to take up the shield of faith in You that protects me from enemy attack (Ephesians 6:16). "For Your righteousness' sake bring my soul out of trouble. In Your mercy cut off my enemies, and destroy all those who afflict my soul; for I am Your servant" (Psalm 143:11-12).

In Jesus' name I pray.

When I cry out to You,
then my enemies will turn back;
this I know, because God is for me.

PSALM 56:9

Prayer Notes

_____

_____

_____

_____

_____

_____

_____

_____

_____

_____

_____

38

Leave the World of His Enemy Entirely

~~~~~~~~~~~~~~~~~~~~~~~~~~~~~~~~~~~~~~~

*L*ord, help me to resist all temptation to live as those who serve the enemy. When tempted, I will worship You because praise invites Your presence in a powerful way and the enemy hates it. Thank You that You are on my side and I need not fear what man can do to me (Psalm 118:6). Thank You that Your commandments "make me wiser than my enemies" (Psalm 119:98). Thank You that no weapon of the enemy formed against me will prosper (Isaiah 54:17). Help me to separate myself from the world in my heart so that I don't follow after anything that is not of You. I know You enable me to do what I cannot do without You.

In Jesus' name I pray.

Whatever is born of God overcomes the world.
And this is the victory that
has overcome the world—our faith.
Who is he who overcomes the world, but he who
believes that Jesus is the Son of God?

1 JOHN 5:4-5

Prayer Notes

_____

_____

_____

_____

_____

_____

_____

_____

_____

_____

_____

39

Long for His Will and His Presence Continuously

~~~~~~

Lord, I long to do Your will at all times. Doing Your will is food for my mind, soul, and spirit that gives me strength and peace. I don't ever want to be outside of Your perfect will for my life, so help me to always look to You for guidance and counsel. Lord Jesus, I know You did not seek Your own will on earth, but the will of Your Father who sent You (John 5:30). Enable me to fully submit my will to our heavenly Father as well. Lord, I pray You will always fill me with the knowledge of Your perfect will (Colossians 1:9). Enable me to live in Your will and Your presence.

In Jesus' name I pray.

Do not be conformed to this world,
but be transformed by the renewing of your mind,
that you may prove what is that
good and acceptable and perfect will of God.

ROMANS 12:2

Prayer Notes

_____

_____

_____

_____

_____

_____

_____

_____

_____

40

Long for His Will and
His Presence Continuously

~~~~~~

Lord, You are life to me, and I cannot live without sensing Your presence in my life. "I spread out my hands to You; my soul longs for You like a thirsty land" (Psalm 143:6). I know that "the upright shall dwell in Your presence" (Psalm 140:13). Help me to do the right thing so that I don't lose that sense of Your presence. I am grateful You never leave or forsake me because Your Spirit dwells within me, but I don't want to do anything to grieve Your Spirit in me or to lose my sense of closeness to You. That means more than life itself. So help me to continuously seek Your precious presence in my life.

In Jesus' name I pray.

As the deer pants for the water brooks,
so pants my soul for You, O God.
My soul thirsts for God, for the living God.

PSALM 42:1-2

Prayer Notes

_____

_____

_____

_____

_____

_____

_____

_____

_____

_____

41

Is Consistently Loving Others Really Possible?

~~~~~~

Lord, I know that without You I don't have it in me to love others the way You want me to. It's only because of Your healing and restoring love guiding me by the power of Your Spirit that I have the capacity and the strength to show love in a life-changing way. I pray You would pour Your love into my heart and give me the ability to love people the way You do. Enable me to always show love in a manner that's pleasing to You. I know that my love for others can reveal Your perfect love within me. Help me to always be available to Your enabling me to do exactly that.

In Jesus' name I pray.

Above all these things put on love,
which is the bond of perfection.

Colossians 3:14

Prayer Notes

_____

_____

_____

_____

_____

_____

_____

_____

_____

42

Is Consistently Loving Others Really Possible?

~~~~~~

Lord, I pray for all believers who are persecuted for their faith. Help those of us who worship in freedom to not forget those who cannot. I don't know how much longer we will be able to worship in freedom ourselves because of evil forces everywhere who have welcomed the anti-Christ spirit into their hearts. They work day and night against those of us who love and serve You, but I hope in Your return. Help us, Your people, not to wait apathetically as if we have no input into this world. Help us to remember that our love and prayers in Your name are always more powerful than their hate. Give us strength to keep praying for and loving others.

In Jesus' name I pray.

*The effective, fervent prayer
of a righteous man avails much.*

JAMES 5:16

Prayer Notes

_____
_____
_____
_____
_____
_____
_____
_____
_____
_____
_____

43

Is Consistently Loving Others Really Possible?

~~~~~~

Lord, help me to obey Your command to love others as You love me. Teach me to live in Your love in such a complete way that this is not a challenge for me but rather a way of life. Enable me to love those who are hard to love. And show me how to better express love for the ones I already love. I know that if I claim to love You, my love extended to others is the proof of that. I know that without love as my motivation I accomplish nothing. I know that love is one of the fruit of the Spirit, and without it in my heart I will not bear fruit in my life.

In Jesus' name I pray.

*This commandment we have from Him:
that he who loves God must love his brother also.*

1 John 4:21

Prayer Notes

_____
_____
_____
_____
_____
_____
_____
_____
_____
_____
_____

44

What if I Can't Always
Be Patient and Kind?

~~~~~~

Lord, I ask You to fill me afresh this day with Your Spirit and Your love. Help me to develop a nature more like Yours. On my own my patience is limited, and my ability to extend love and kindness to others is imperfect at best. I know that whatever I do or say without Your love in my heart is meaningless and accomplishes nothing. Enable me to say and do everything from a heart that has been melded and molded to more resemble Yours. I want to be known as Your disciple, and that cannot happen if I don't have love for my brothers and sisters in Christ. Fill me with Your Spirit of love so that it flows from me to them.

In Jesus' name I pray.

A new commandment I give to you,
that you love one another;
as I have loved you, that you also love one another.
By this all will know that you are My disciples,
if you have love for one another.

JOHN 13:34-35

Prayer Notes

_____

_____

_____

_____

_____

_____

_____

_____

_____

_____

45

What if I Can't Always Be Patient and Kind?

~~~~~~

Lord, I lift my heart to You and ask You to fill it with Your patience, mercy, and kindness. Show me each day who especially needs an act or word of kindness from me and what that should be. Make me sensitive to the needs of others, and give me sensitivity to Your Spirit speaking to my heart and guiding me in this. I know that patience, kindness, and love are all connected (2 Peter 1:7). There are great rewards when I extend them to other people. Help me to add to my faith virtue, knowledge, self-control, perseverance, godliness, brotherly kindness, and love. You know I cannot do this without Your Spirit of love in me.

In Jesus' name I pray.

Add to your faith virtue,
to virtue knowledge,
to knowledge self-control,
to self-control perseverance,
to perseverance godliness,
to godliness brotherly kindness,
and to brotherly kindness love.

2 Peter 1:5-7

Prayer Notes

_____

_____

_____

_____

_____

_____

_____

_____

_____

46

What if I Can't Always Be Patient and Kind?

~~~~~~

Lord, help me to be merciful and forgiving to others. Enable me to be patient, tolerant, bighearted, understanding, steadfast, amicable, tenderhearted, considerate, sensitive, unwearied, and compassionate with other people, just as You are with me. I pray You will enable me to be kind, helpful, forgiving, friendly, peaceable, agreeable, gracious, warmhearted, sensitive, gentle, and affable toward everyone. Lord, You know I cannot do this on my own. My feelings get hurt and I can become angry, resentful, tired, depleted, selfish, and unwilling to forgive. Being always patient and kind is something I must actively pursue—but I cannot do that without You. Only with You helping me can I love others the way You do and glorify You in the process.

In Jesus' name I pray.

*Let your light so shine before men,
that they may see your good works and glorify
your Father in heaven.*

Matthew 5:16

Prayer Notes

_____

_____

_____

_____

_____

_____

_____

_____

_____

_____

_____

47

In What Ways Do I
Reveal a Lack of Love?

~~~~~~

Lord, help me to recognize anything in me that reveals a lack of love in my heart for others. Teach me to understand what love *is* by also understanding what love is *not*. Help me to never envy others, but to be happy for all that they *have* or *are*. Thank You that You have given me so much for which I am grateful. Keep me from ever flaunting, parading, or drawing attention to myself. Make me aware of the way I am presenting myself to others so that I do not make anyone feel bad instead of loved. Help me to seek other people's well-being over my own. I realize that is consistently impossible without Your enabling me.

In Jesus' name I pray.

Let no one seek his own,
but each one the other's well-being.

1 Corinthians 10:24

Prayer Notes

_____

_____

_____

_____

_____

_____

_____

_____

_____

_____

48

In What Ways Do I Reveal a Lack of Love?

*L*ord, help me to want what *You* want more than what *I* want. Keep me from being easily provoked, irritated, or hurt. Remove from my heart all pride. I know it can only lead to destruction because it's blatant rebellion against You. Save me from ever becoming haughty and aligning myself with the enemy. Stop me from becoming wise in my own eyes because I know You are merciful to humble people and You bring down those who are haughty (Psalm 18:27). Keep me from showing a lack of love to others by being conceited, boastful, condescending, or presumptuous. Help me to instead be humble, teachable, submissive, and not thinking I can do all of this without Your help.

In Jesus' name I pray.

LORD, You have heard the desire of the humble;
You will prepare their heart;
You will cause Your ear to hear.

PSALM 10:17

Prayer Notes

_____

_____

_____

_____

_____

_____

_____

_____

_____

_____

49

In What Ways Do I Reveal a Lack of Love?

~~~~~~

Lord, give me a heart that is sensitive to others so that I am never rude or selfish. Fill my heart and mind with Your truth so that I never entertain evil thoughts. Keep me from celebrating another's bad news or downfall. Help me to discard any offense from an irritating person so I can let it go and not carry it like a burden. Teach me to love others in the way You want me to, and to reject all indications of lovelessness in me. Help me to be kind and affectionate to everyone and never be heavy-handed, offensive, or impolite. I pray I will always recognize pride in myself so it will find no place in me.

In Jesus' name I pray.

*Be kindly affectionate to one another
with brotherly love,
in honor giving preference to one another;
not lagging in diligence, fervent in spirit,
serving the Lord.*

ROMANS 12:10-11

Prayer Notes

_____

_____

_____

_____

_____

_____

_____

_____

_____

_____

_____

50

How Will Others Know
I Am God's?

*L*ord, Your Word says that it is good and pleasant for all of us who love You to live together in unity (Psalm 133:1). And that we should love one another, for when we love You and love others, it shows that we truly *know* You (1 John 4:7). Help me to be a uniter and not a divider. Help me to be a peacemaker and not a troublemaker, a bridgemaker and not a destroyer. I know there are great blessings for those who are all that. Whenever there are divisions between others, or between me and others, give me the ability to bring people together with the words I say.

In Jesus' name I pray.

Blessed are the peacemakers,
for they shall be called sons of God.

MATTHEW 5:9

Prayer Notes

_____

_____

_____

_____

_____

_____

_____

_____

_____

_____

_____

51

How Will Others Know
I Am God's?

~~~~~~

Lord, teach me to speak words that lift up and bring love and peace—words that edify and cause people to love You more. Enable me to speak only that which is true, righteous, and godly. Keep me from being a negative complainer. Your Word says that godly speech brings a long, good life (Psalm 34:12-13). Help me to speak the truth about what constitutes a long, good life for others. Enable me to communicate Your love to them in every way possible. I know that part of loving others is being able to drop a matter and just let it go. That's hard to do sometimes, and I need Your help to enable me to recover and quickly move on.

In Jesus' name I pray.

*Though I speak with the tongues of men
and of angels, but have not love,
I have become sounding brass
or a clanging cymbal.*

1 Corinthians 13:1

Prayer Notes

_____

_____

_____

_____

_____

_____

_____

_____

_____

_____

_____

52

How Will Others Know
I Am God's?

~~~~~~

*L*ord, I pray I will be known for my love for You and for other people (John 13:35). I pray that even unbelievers will know me by my love expressed to them in kindness and thoughtfulness. I pray they will be attracted to You because of it. Teach me how to "pursue love"—not only to receive it, but to look to You for the opportunities You have opened to me to show it to others (1 Corinthians 14:1). Teach me how to pray to that end so I can extend Your love to those who are dividers. Enable us all to love one another with a pure heart (1 Peter 1:22). I want to be known as Your friend and disciple.

In Jesus' name I pray.

By this all will know that you are My disciples,
if you have love for one another.

JOHN 13:35

Prayer Notes

_____

_____

_____

_____

_____

_____

_____

_____

_____

_____

_____

53

Isn't It Selfish to Learn to Love Myself?

~~~~~~

Lord, thank You that You love me and that You made me for Your purposes. Help me to appreciate all You have put in me. Enable me to recognize the gifts You have given me to be used for Your glory. Teach me to see the good in me that I'm not seeing and help me to reject the self-criticism I focus on. Teach me to love You more and love myself better so I can express love to others with greater clarity. Help me to seek wisdom that comes only from You because I care enough about myself to become all You made me to be. Help me to understand how much You love me and what You see in me.

In Jesus' name I pray.

He who gets wisdom loves his own soul;
he who keeps understanding will find good.

PROVERBS 19:8

Prayer Notes

_____

_____

_____

_____

_____

_____

_____

_____

_____

_____

_____

54

Isn't It Selfish to Learn to Love Myself?

~~~~~~

Lord, I confess any feelings I have about my life that are negative and critical. You are in charge of my life, and I trust You to bring good into it. Give me wisdom to see the great things You have put in me that will be used for Your glory. Help me to love others as You have taught me to love myself—that is, with great appreciation for Your work in me and in them. I know that when I love You, myself, and others that this is the fulfillment of the law (Romans 13:10). I do not want to short-circuit that in any way. I pray that everything I think and say will please You.

In Jesus' name I pray.

Let the words of my mouth
and the meditation of my heart
be acceptable in Your sight, O LORD,
my strength and my Redeemer.

PSALM 19:14

Prayer Notes

_____

_____

_____

_____

_____

_____

_____

_____

_____

_____

_____

_____

55

Isn't It Selfish to
Learn to Love Myself?

~~~~~~

Lord, help me to "pursue righteousness, godliness, faith, love, patience, gentleness" because they are beautiful in Your eyes and pleasing to You (1 Timothy 6:11). Lord, You are beautiful and wonderful and lovely and attractive and desirable. Let all that You are shine through all that I am. Help me to love myself in a way that doesn't say, "I am great," but rather says, "You are great and You are in me making me more like You every day." Help me to walk with You in a way that is always worthy of my calling and reflects who You made me to be. Help me to be more patient with myself and not critical so that I am not expecting things of myself that You do not.

In Jesus' name I pray.

Walk worthy of the calling with which you were
called, with all lowliness and gentleness, with
longsuffering, bearing with one another in love.

EPHESIANS 4:1-2

Prayer Notes

_____

_____

_____

_____

_____

_____

_____

_____

_____

_____

_____

56

What if I'm Unable to Bear, Believe, Hope, and Endure All Things?

~~~~~~

Lord, help me to *bear* all things when it comes to loving others. I know You will not call me to go beyond what I can bear because it is You who calls me and sustains me. Uphold me so I have strength to help others and stand with them as they go through trials. Help me to lend support, bolster up, put up with, and uphold. Help me to *believe* all things by suspending any disbelief I have in me regarding others. If I cannot believe for the best in them, I can believe for *Your* best for them. Help me to give them the benefit of the doubt. Help me to encourage them as You have encouraged me.

In Jesus' name I pray.

*Whatever things you ask in prayer,
believing, you will receive.*

MATTHEW 21:22

Prayer Notes

_____

_____

_____

_____

_____

_____

_____

_____

_____

_____

_____

_____

57

What if I'm Unable to Bear, Believe, Hope, and Endure All Things?

~~~~~~

*L*ord, help me to *hope* all things for others because my hope for them is in You. Just as I never suspend my hope in You, help me to not lose hope in other people either. Help me to not write people off who have disappointed me or seem to never respond to the hope You have for them. Help me to live in hopeful anticipation of what You will do and cheerful expectancy of Your imminent blessings. Teach me to expect good things because of all You have promised to those who love You. I have courage because I know You will strengthen my heart because my hope is in You (Psalm 31:24).

In Jesus' name I pray.

Be of good courage,
and He shall strengthen your heart,
all you who hope in the LORD.

PSALM 31:24

Prayer Notes

_____

_____

_____

_____

_____

_____

_____

_____

_____

_____

_____

_____

What if I'm Unable to Bear, Believe, Hope, and Endure All Things?

~~~~~~

Lord, enable me to *endure* the things You have called me to as a sign of love for others. Help me to persevere in prayer for them and encourage them to stay true to You and Your Word and the promises You have given us all. Help me to keep going and trying again after someone has rejected Your love and mine. Help me to go the distance with the ones You have instructed me to do so. I don't want to be a person who only endures for a while (Matthew 13:21). I want to stay the course with You so I can stay the course with others to whom You lead me to reveal Your love.

In Jesus' name I pray.

Let us lay aside every weight, and the sin which so easily ensnares us, and let us run with endurance the race that is set before us, looking unto Jesus, the author and finisher of our faith.

Hebrews 12:1-2

Prayer Notes

_____

_____

_____

_____

_____

_____

_____

_____

_____

59

How Can I Show Love
in Every Situation?

~~~~~~

*L*ord, I pursue love just as I pursue You, because You are love and Your love never fails. Fill my heart so full of Your love that it overflows to others. Enable me to show Your love in every situation. I depend on You for guidance with that. Lead me by Your Holy Spirit to make decisions regarding what is always pleasing to You. I don't want to interfere with what You are doing in another's life. I don't want to move in the flesh, but instead be led by Your Spirit in all I do and say. Help me to seek Your will in every situation and with each person, and not assume I know what to do in every case.

In Jesus' name I pray.

This is the message that you
heard from the beginning,
that we should love one another.

1 John 3:11

Prayer Notes

_____

_____

_____

_____

_____

_____

_____

_____

_____

_____

_____

60

How Can I Show Love in Every Situation?

~~~~~~

*L*ord, teach me to love others with the love in my heart that comes from You. I know that "the mouth of the righteous brings forth wisdom" and "the lips of the righteous know what is acceptable" (Proverbs 10:31-32). Help me to know words that are wise and acceptable all the time. I know that "in the multitude of words sin is not lacking, but he who restrains his lips is wise," so make my words to be valuable and edifying to others and never meaningless (Proverbs 10:19-20). I know that can only happen by Your Spirit of love working in and through me. Enable me as only You can do to not show a lack of love in any way.

In Jesus' name I pray.

May our Lord Jesus Christ Himself,
and our God and Father,
who has loved us and given us everlasting
consolation and good hope by grace,
comfort your hearts and establish you in
every good word and work.

2 THESSALONIANS 2:16-17

Prayer Notes

_____

_____

_____

_____

_____

_____

_____

_____

_____

_____

Other Books by Stormie Omartian

Lead Me, Holy Spirit

The Holy Spirit wants those who know Him to hear when He speaks to their heart, soul, and spirit. He wants to help believers enter into the relationship with God they yearn for, the wholeness and freedom God has for them, and the place of safety they can only find by following His leading to the center of His perfect will.

Prayer Warrior

For every Christian who wants a meaningful prayer life that is more than just asking for blessings, bestselling author Stormie Omartian shows you how to pray with strength and purpose—prayers resulting in great victory, not only personally but also in advancing God's kingdom and glory.

The Power of a Praying Wife® Devotional

In 100 uplifting devotions and prayers written just for this book, Stormie offers a praying wife fresh ways to pray for her husband, herself, and her marriage. These easy-to-read devotions will increase any wife's understanding, strength, and peace, and provide her with help and perspective on the situations and challenges she faces.

The Power of Praying® for Your Adult Children

In this follow-up to *The Power of a Praying® Parent*, Stormie addresses areas of concern you may have for your grown children and shares how to effectively lift them up to God. It doesn't matter how young or old they are, you can rest in the power of God working through your prayers for them.